Splinters
in my
pride

Splinters in my pride

by Marilee Zdenek

WORD BOOKS
PUBLISHER

books by Marilee Zdenek

SPLINTERS IN MY PRIDE
SOMEONE SPECIAL

and in collaboration with Marge Champion

GOD IS A VERB!
CATCH THE NEW WIND

SPLINTERS IN MY PRIDE

Copyright © 1979 by Marilee Zdenek
All rights reserved.

ISBN 0-8499-0118-9
Library of Congress Catalog Card Number: 79-63936

Printed in the United States of America

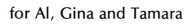

for Al, Gina and Tamara

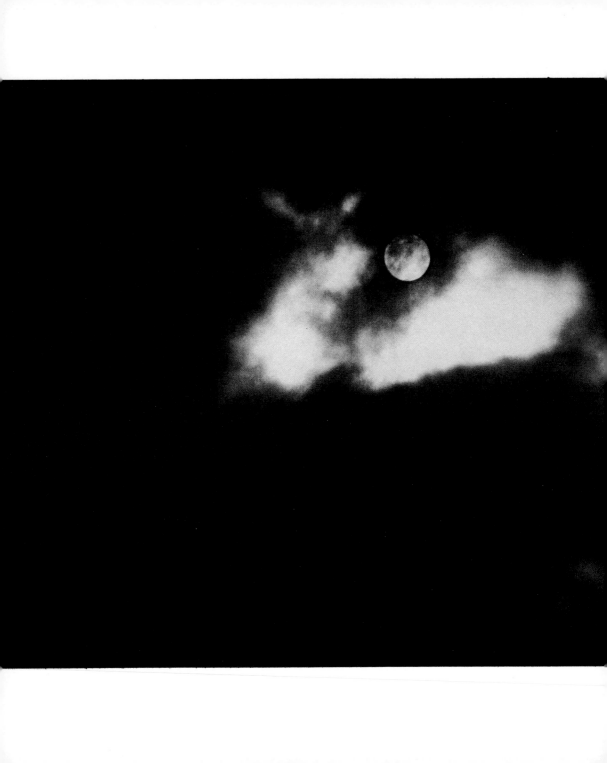

I've written miles of words;
placed end to end,
they stretch across the landscape of my years,
measuring feelings and moods,
changes of heart and mind.

Good times merge with hard
and both survive,
only pretending to pass away with time—

Like yesterday,
which never really dies,
but only changes form.

Part I

The Green Rose

There's a cottage that lives in the woods
And the woods are only
Three acres small
And grow in the middle
Of the San Fernando Valley.

No one knows how it came to be
That such a place could grow there,
In the dusty basin,
On the dreary side of Los Angeles,
But there it is.

Oak and Walnut trees stretch out,
Touching branches over the creek
That flows by the cottage—when it rains.

Ferns with names I've never heard
And striped tulips and pink lilies
And even a green rose live there.

A biologist once said there was no such thing as a green rose—
Until he got pricked by its thorns.
He had to bleed a little
To know what was real.

Ethics ran high in our home;
A lie was tantamount to treason.
Everyone told the truth in our home—
About everything
Except feelings.

"A lady never shows her temper,"
"Big girls don't cry,"
"Nice girls don't think that way,"
"Now where's that pretty smile?"

I didn't cheat in school,
Or take what wasn't mine,
But, oh how many times I lied
About the feelings
I hid inside.

I knew a girl when she was nine and she was very tall for her age. She hated her legs, which she thought were too long, and her feet, which she thought were too big, and her freckles, which she believed were quite ugly.

A woman, who lived in her block, organized a parade— rather grandly as neighborhood parades go—and all the children were given parts and costumes except for this one girl who was left out and didn't know why. So she went to the woman and begged to be included and finally the woman said yes. But she wouldn't let the girl be anything pretty like she needed to be. If she was going to be in the parade, she would have to be the fat lady because that was the only costume left.

It was hard for her to do that. But she did. She played the part and walked down the street wearing layer upon layer of padding and huge pendulous breasts and heavy purple lipstick.

The people laughed and laughed. She found that it was easier to hide her tears if she acted silly and made faces and tried to pretend that she was laughing too.

Everyone said what a good sport she was. Everyone said she looked so funny, they laughed until they cried. Everyone said she was so good she should grow up to be an actress.

No one seemed to know that she already was.

I've watched you stumbling
On a path that leads to nowhere
And I've seen your pain
Made tangible in tears.
I've watched you take the same steps before
And now again.

What draws you there?

What fascination pulls you back
To a place that wounds?
Are you working something through
Each time you go?
What holds you there—
Do you know?

Long ago, I asked my parents
    (using other words)
    "Am I of value? Does my life have meaning?"
Then I asked my teachers,
    later, directors and editors,
    husband and friends—
    "Am I of value? Does my life have meaning?"
Then I asked God and God said "Yes."
And that should have finished it.

But it didn't.

Once I knew a little girl who spent her own money to buy a box of gold stars and stuck every one of them on a piece of paper that had her name at the top.

Success is a slippery place at best—
But wouldn't it feel fine
Just to slither around there
For a time?

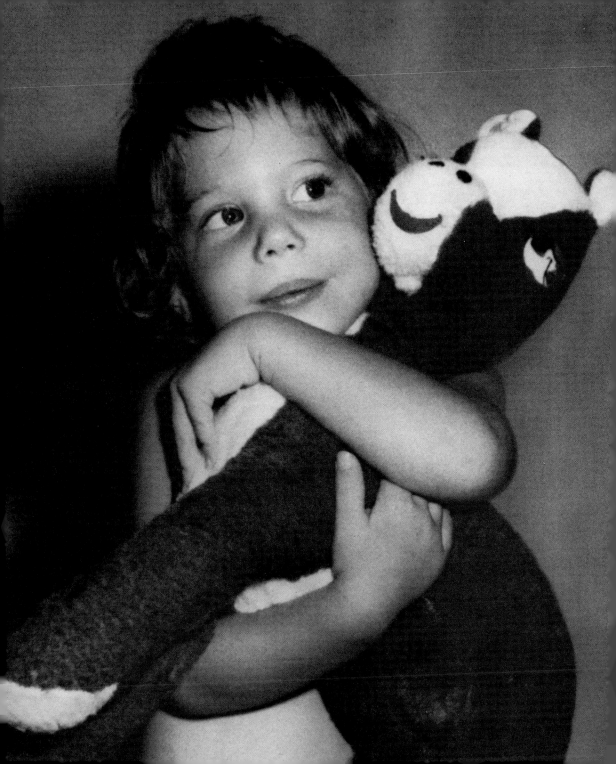

There was a young lady of three, who was vitally interested in physiology. In the universal game of Show and Tell, she made a remarkable discovery. For when a certain young man removed his pants, not only did he display his natural endowment, but also his behind—with a rash—which his mother had treated with purple ointment. He didn't explain how his fanny got so colorful, and she didn't ask. She didn't ask how the other side of him got that way either—some things just *are,* that's all.

And when the little girl shared this worldly knowledge with her friends, she had more news to tell than anyone, for she had discovered that not only do they have fancy accouterments in front, but all little boys have purple bottoms.

I was a good mother then—
When all you needed was love,
A full breast
And a dry bottom.

I was a good mother later—
When you toddled around your circumscribed world
Needing attention
And a watchful eye.

Now you're seventeen
And I'm not sure what you need
But I'm sure it isn't me.
And I'm not sure at all
What being a good mother means.

I would take back the accusations if I could.
I would erase the words with wishes
Trade temper for patience
Turn lectures to listening
I would.

Much I would undo, if wishes could.

It's hard to raise children when you're a constant seeker (and rather hard on the children too, I suppose) because the rules keep changing as you outgrow the things you believed to be true and discover other things which are also true. In a world where only God isn't changing, sometimes it takes some doing just to keep things in focus.

It's only one more splinter in my pride—
So I WILL NOT be defensive,
I decided.
What does it matter if you say
That Janie's mom is skinny,
And Gretchen's mom can ski,
And Lisa's mom's a super cook
And—
> WHATDOYOUMEAN
> NO OTHER MOTHER
> SITS AROUND
> WASTING HER TIME
> JUST WRITING BOOKS!

Reach for any star you want, my child,
Any star at all.
The sky is full of dreams for the plucking.
Choose one,
Or more,
The sky has no limit.

Dream high, my child,
Let your fantasies run wild with what could be.
Watch the falling star—
A dream descending—
Catch it as it flies,
It's bad luck to pick your wishes off the ground.

It was hard to let you go:
To watch womanhood reach out and snatch you
Long before the mothering was done.
But if God listened to mothers and gave in,
Would the time for turning loose of daughters ever come?

It was hard when you went away—
For how was I to know
The serendipity of letting go
Would be seeing you come home again
And meeting in a new way
Woman to woman—
Friend to friend.

Part II

Stormy Morning Sky

Where were you when my world fell apart—
When the earth split beneath me
And a lifetime of dreams
Slipped into oblivion?

I don't know where you were
But it wasn't here.

Being at one with the total self,
Accepting all that has been and will be,
Knowing that pain is not alien to joy
But the dark thread enriching the pale tapestry . . .
Isn't easy.

Sometimes, poems won't come when called
With words like
Work
Struggle
Grit
Hurry.

Sometimes, poems want to be coaxed
Like children and puppies
Who hide beneath the bed—
Waiting for words like
Whisper
And wispy
And tender
And yes.

Sometimes poems want to rest under a tree
Staring at the sky awhile
Finding faces in the twig patterns
And leaves.

I trust that.
They may know their needs
Better than I know mine.
Poems have strong wills
That defy manipulation.

I wish I did.

A young girl was given a talent. And she knew that the gift required time and commitment. But her days were filled with things she had to do, and there were also things she loved to do, and still more things that she was told she really *ought* to do. So her talent suffered from lack of use.

She grew to be a woman, loved a man. Loved the children their love produced. Still, she worried about the talent that was rarely used, which lay like a pale and fragile child in a distant room, who called to her from time to time in a voice that she could barely hear above the sound of all the things she had to do.

The woman had a dream one night and saw herself as old and worn. She reached for her talent, for now she had time: there wasn't much that she had to get done anymore. But the talent had died.

And the old woman mourned.

Morning came. Echoes of the dream remained.

"The choice is mine," the woman said.

And *made* the time she didn't have.

Would you like for me to tell you
What I think—
Or would you like for me to tell you
What I feel?
They're not the same thing, you know.

Or did you.

It is this that I crave:
  a place to be
  to grow
  season to season
  tomorrow rooted in today
  tendrils reaching through the past
  growing deeper into time
  stretching higher into space
  a world of order
  a sense of place.

        A woman who fears the tremor
        shouldn't settle on the fault
        or plant herself where soil's been known to shift.
        My life it seems is always set in change
        and growth must come within the midst of this.

                With an angry cry protesting—
                then accepting—
                the severing from all that's been,
                with roots in pocket
                I move on.
                Again.

Racing in parallel lines—fast as
Worms we inch our way
Down freeways night and day.

Progressing—
So they say.

Phoney-faced lady,
Chic—oh yes!
Starched your manners,
Ironed your smile across your
Mask.
Calm as the driven
Stone you are—
Never a temper out of place.
A place for everything
But no place for feelings,
Poor, dear, phoney-faced lady—
Won't you risk
One belly laugh
One charitable guffaw
Or one real tear
For such a good cause
As living?

Come on, Caterpillar—
Emerge and fly!
Beware of silk that spins too tight a case
Bang your wings against the steel world
Shatter iron with gossamer touch
Spread mottled golden tissue dreams
Against this stormy morning sky
And fly!

Looking backward at ninety,
Looking forward to heaven—
You're getting ready to move
Out of one life-zone
Into another.

You speak of death like it's the vacation you've been promised
But never taken;
Like people you love are waiting there
And you're holding up the party;
Like God himself is fitting you with dancing shoes,
Feet that won't hurt,
And eyes that can see again.

Years ago, I remember,
"Grandmother" had too formal a sound,
So I gave you love-names
And made up songs
And stories in your honor.

I guess I still do.

I'm going to miss you.

All those times, before I found the
sun, much less the
rainbow, you stayed close and warmed my lonely
spirit with your touch. Dear special friend—
without you,
how cold and black the
darkness would have been.

I've loved and sorrowed, despaired and survived.
I've bumped head-on into my own humanity time after time.

Getting in touch with that humanity wasn't an easy thing for me. Nor is it for any of us who were raised to excel, to make contributions to the world, to rise above anger and jealousy and all of those other things that none of us ever rise above.

I don't write about rising above; I write about going through. In the going through comes the victory—or at least the survival.

I've survived because of prayer, which I believe in, and therapy, which I also believe in, and love—which I believe in most of all.

All the loves that we love are part of the same love.
All the deaths that we live through are part of the same dying.
And while we laugh or cry for different reasons,
The sound of happiness is much the same everywhere.
And tears, wept for whatever reason,
Always taste of salt.

I am most of the nameless people in this book.
Are you?

Part III

The Sound of Shadows Touching

What Huckleberry children we were that summer—
Roaming the meadows, swimming the streams,
Exploring our feelings, finding
Ourselves.
Side by side we lay on a green clover bed,
Almost touching—
But not quite.
You said I was your best girl—
Only girl, always girl,
Almost touching — but not quite.
You felt the softness
Of the pussy willow stalk,
Rolling the velvet buds
Back and forth
Between your fingers
As you talked—
Slowly, slowly,
As you talked.
You sucked on the honeysuckle stem,
Not daring to find my lips and take the honey
That lay beneath my tongue.
Not touching, not touching, not yet.
Oh, my sandy-haired, almost lover—
Where did you go
At the end of summer?

You take both my hands in yours
in silence
just your fingers tracing
patterns of lovemaking
on my palms
erasing everything but
the two of us
touch to touch
lifelines embracing
needs merging
hands speaking a language
words don't know. Promising
more.
Oh!

"Watch your head," you said,
As I stepped aboard your yacht.
I took care
Not to hurt my head,
It was my heart
I forgot to watch.

There you sit—
Surrounded by that invisible wall
You constructed
To keep me out.
Isn't it lonely in that fortress
By yourself?

It's rumored that the sun never shines
Behind self-made walls.
I can't bear to see you
Cold
When I have so much
Warm
To share. Come on—
I only want to touch
My life to yours
For a moment or two.

Unless of course,
You ask me
To stay
Longer.

You can play it safe
And keep your life tidy,
Take all of your risks
And vault them into the
Bank.

Or you can say you love me—
And wait to see what happens.

We walked the beach when our love was new—
    and heard the husky laughter of the sea,
    like a zany clown
    summersaulting to the shore,
    springing from the rocks
    to chase the tide once more.
    The wind and the cypress danced upon the cliff,
    and everywhere we looked
    there was happiness and love.

I walked the beach when you went away—
    and heard the longing whisper of the sea,
    like an anxious lover
    rushing to fondle the shore
    and kiss the rocks
    with searching
    silver tongue.
    The wind caressed the cypress on the cliff,
    and everywhere I looked
    there were memories of love.

If I rub my thoughts against you, softly,
Like the touch of butterfly wings,
Will you feel the fluttering of my fantasies
Upon your body?
If I rub my thoughts against you, tenderly,
Like the moth caressing the tip of the flower
That stands tall in the grassy meadow,
Will you think of the flower and of me?
Will you think of me
Wanting you—
And then of the flower,
Blooming gloriously in the sun
Before the wilting?

You have the
Gentlest hands, the
Tenderest touch—
Like clouds caressing
Mountain tops.

Before the storm.

I thought I knew you
After all these years of intertwining lives
Binding us dream to dream.
Then I saw the house you lived in
Once upon a time—
The tree you climbed
The place you hid.
I heard your boy-laugh
Felt your roots
Touched your childhood
Dusty with years.
I know you better now, my love—
I know you closer than I did.

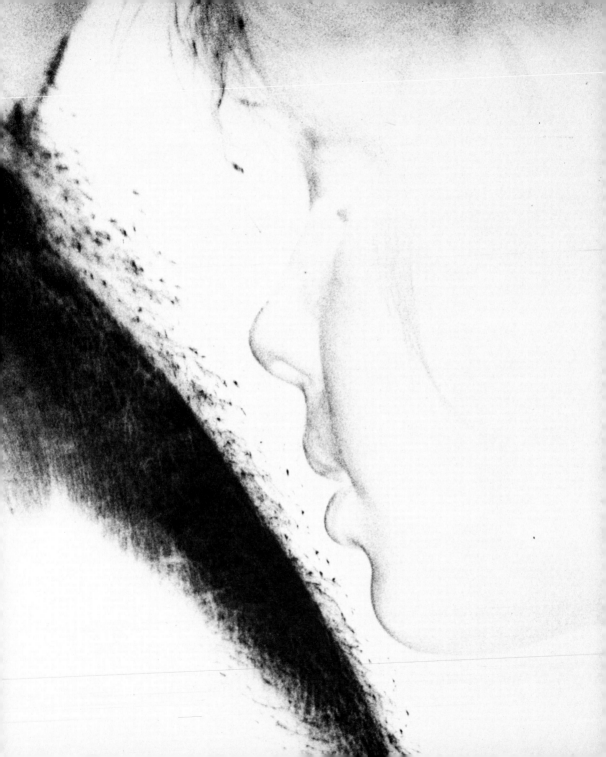

We meet in dreams
Our thoughts embracing.
I reach for you across the pillow
And the distance of a thousand miles.
Hold me in your thoughts awhile,
Whisper that you love me
And listen—
For the sound of shadows—
Touching.

Sharing our bodies
      is one kind of close.
Sharing our secret thoughts
      is another.

Taking the risk of
      stripping bare the ego,
      getting down to who we are—
            and still feeling loved—
            and then making love,
                is the best there is.

Come close.

I trust you.

IN APPRECIATION. . . . .

I want to thank my family most of all: my husband, Al—my daughters, Gina and Tamara. Living in a home where a book is in the birth cycle involves some flexibility on everyone's part. I appreciate their help and their willingness to let me include the poems that deal with our relationships—our struggles as well as our joys.

I took most of the photographs for *Splinters in My Pride,* using family and friends as models. A few exceptions: Al photographed the glacier in Canada and my picture for the back jacket. He also took that dejected shot of Tamara, years ago, when we wouldn't let her ride on a horse in the desert by herself (p. 20).

Gina took the street scene in Spain and Tamara photographed the ocean. Kay Carson took pictures of the children (pp. 12 and 24) and David Worth took the last picture in the book—of Al's hands and mine.

It was David who encouraged me to publish my pictures—and he taught me some valuable things about photography along the way.

I also want to thank Sheryl and Biff Sherman for the title of this book and I'm especially grateful to Baylis and Perla who began it all with love.